Modern Proverbs More Quotes, Quips and Questions

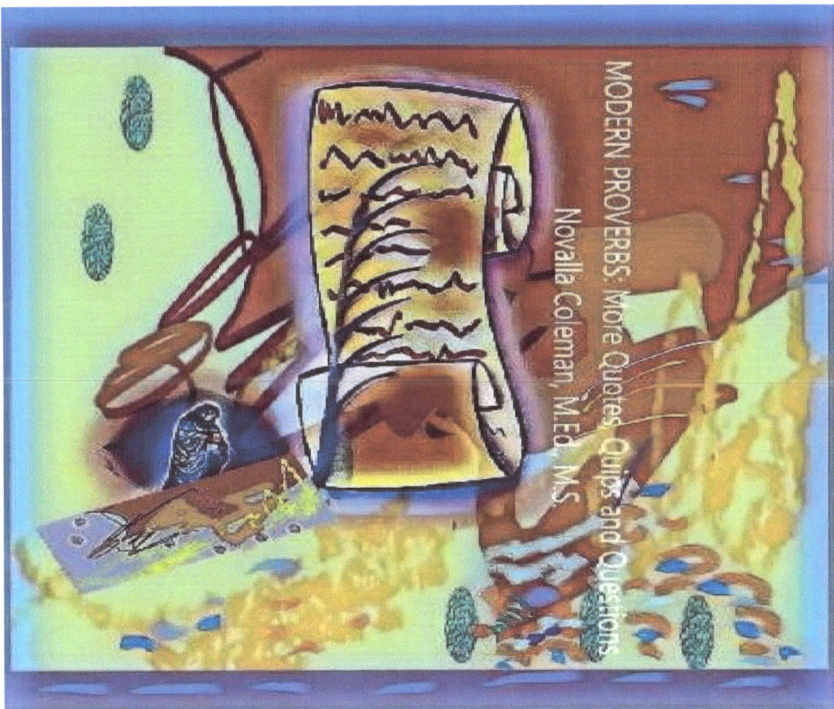

MODERN PROVERBS: More Quotes, Quips and Questions
Novalla Coleman, M.Ed., M.S.

Novalla Coleman, M.Ed., M.S.

Disclaimer

Author, Novalla Coleman, affiliated entities and/or corporations connected to this book and the contents thereof do not intend to replace professional advice or counsel in any area including but not limited to legal, financial, marital, medical, spiritual, psychological, or employment. Please seek a licensed professional, if help is required.

Novalla Coleman and Team

Modern Proverbs: More Quotes, Quips and Questions

We all need wisdom. Thus, it matters not what our station in life is, we always need wisdom for life's journey and for the inevitable challenges, which we all must face. Here is proof.....Wisdom is the principal thing; therefore get wisdom: and with all thy getting, get understanding. Proverbs 4:7 KJV Also…But be ye doers of the word, and not hearers only, deceiving your own selves. For if any be a hearer of the word, and not a doer, he is like unto a man beholding his natural face in a glass: For he beholdeth himself, and goeth his way, and Straight-way forgetteth what manner of man he was. Finally…But whoso looketh into the perfect law of liberty, and continueth therein, he being not a forgetful hearer, but a doer of the work, this man shall be blessed in his deed. James 1:22-25 KJV

Dedication

This book is dedicated to my children, my grandchildren and my dreamer comrades. You are possibilities. Keep dreaming. Keep moving forward into your Divine destiny. Never GIVE UP!

Novalla Coleman, M.Ed., M.S.

Modern Proverbs
More Quotes, Quips and Questions

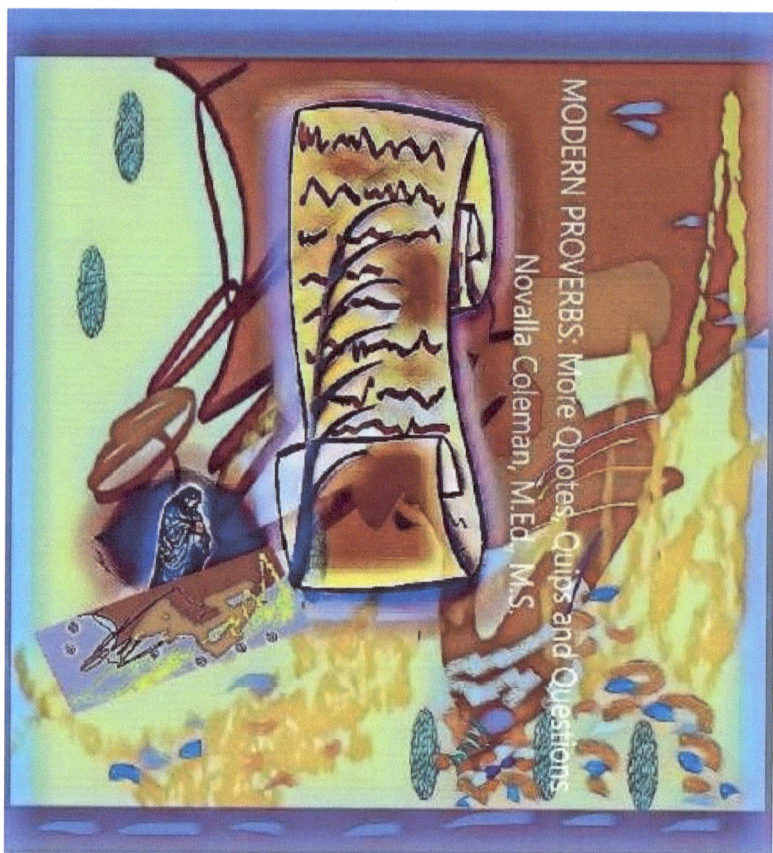

Table of Contents

Modern Proverbs:

More Quotes, Quips and Questions

Introduction

A proverb, based on an online search, is a short pithy saying in general use, stating a general truth or piece of advice. The word proverb has several synonyms. Here is an abbreviated list, which includes the words saying, adage, saw, maxim, axiom, motto, bon mot, aphorism, and precept.

To live a successful life on this earth requires wisdom. True wisdom comes from God and it is the Lord's wisdom from His word and the wise counsel of others (those who have demonstrated wisdom), which can bring deliverance, success, health, family tranquility, and emotional healing. In addition, wisdom can lead into appropriate and timely action for life decisions. Say what you will, but God's divine wisdom should not be taken lightly nor for granted. Because the Lord's wisdom is in written form (His word, the Bible), all can benefit from it, to help with living a successful life. The key is to make right and divine decisions based on wise counsel, which can be found in the Word of God; the Bible, and in some cases, from other wise human beings.

The quotes book, *Modern Proverbs: More Quotes, Quips, and Questions,* was authored by Novalla Coleman and inspired by God. *Modern Proverbs: More Quotes, Quips, and Questions* is Novalla Coleman's second book pertaining to quotes and wisdom. *Modern Proverbs: More Quotes, Quips, and Questions* draws from the major themes of wisdom and universal applicability.

Enlightened ones know the Lord gives wisdom to those who ask for wisdom. And HE gives liberally, as well. It is through HIS word and HIS Holy Spirit that HE gives guidance. So, all honor goes to the Infinite, Unlimited, Abba Father, El-Shaddai, Yahweh, Jehovah, Adonai, the I AM that I AM, the One, true and living God, Elohim, and Jehovah-Shammah as HE enabled Novalla Coleman to capture wise snippets, sayings, quotes, quips, thoughts, and poignant vignettes so that they could be penned here in *Modern Proverbs:* More Quotes, Quips, and Questions.

Modern Proverbs: More Quotes, Quips, and Questions is based on biblical principles, which can be seen throughout the book.

Novalla Coleman's prayer is that readers begin to hold their decisions up to God's word as a mirror. Remember, every decision touches someone else's life.

Come delve into *Modern Proverbs: More Quotes, Quips, and Questions* because wisdom is still.....the principle thing!

Chapter 1: God Connection

Stay in the Vine

I am the vine, ye are the branches: He that abideth in me, and I in him, the same bringeth forth much fruit: for without me ye can do nothing. *John 15:5 KJV*

And why do human beings disconnect from God, the Lord and the Lord Jesus Christ? Could it be that human beings, while living in a feeling of superiority, began to believe that they themselves have all the answers and as such, they look to themselves alone and feebly attempt to leave God out? This is, of course, not wise, in that, He, God, is everywhere present at the same time. He is almighty. He is the beginning and the end, the first and the last, is He. Soon, human beings discover that He is inescapable. However, when human beings come to their right mind, they begin to understand that Jesus is the answer. In the future, move towards God and not away from HIM.

In the vine.....I understand this to mean, I am to remain connected to **I am God**, *the creator of the whole earth, and with that connection, I am and will continue to produce in and for this life, while I wisely prepare for the everlasting future in Glory. The crux of the matter is that without* **I am God**, *I can do nothing. This reminds me of one of the forefathers, namely, Jacob, Isaac's son, who worked for Laban, his father-in-law, all those years to marry Rachel. God gave him one idea. He followed the divine instructions (wisdom) and this one thing caused the livestock to reproduce exponentially. When we become and remain connected to the Divine ONE, we leave earthly rules and regulations behind. It all comes from God!*

An unopened bible is like an unopened gift. It does the recipient no good and belittles the giver's efforts.

When you do little and you could do lots, you help no one. God is not pleased with your performance. You are still in disobedience. Remember the man with one talent.

Jesus is the great fixer. His love drew me like an elixir. His love is good. Oh, taste and see that the Lord is good.

Seeking the Lord must be for a deeper relationship with Him, not for prosperity alone.

The word of God can be a preview of coming attractions.

The Word of the Lord is an equalizer.

The Word of the Lord is a protector: a personal security detail.

God gives His Word as a grand and divine plan. I ask for what I will and according to my faith, it is done unto me.

The Word of the Lord is an unrivaled creative force.

The Word of the Lord is a reoccurring commercial segment for coming attractions.

The Word of the Lord is like a flood lamp with one million candle light power.

The Word of the Lord can see through the darkness, break down walls, cut through a mountain, raise the dead, and turn barrenness into fertility.

The Word of the Lord is a personal defense attorney.

The Word of the Lord places everyone on level ground. It is called trusting in the Lord with all thine heart.

The Word of the Lord is God's rainbow of revival.

I wonder about parents who name their children after great men or women of the bible like Abraham, Noah, David, Deborah, Moses, and Jesus. Parents please pour into them so they measure up to the name!

The Word of the Lord is a purifier.

Accept the Lord. He has already accepted you.

The Word of the Lord is like a city guidebook.

In Christ, I don't have to change, but I need to be willing to change.

Awakened to ….who God is and His word, who you are in God, your gifts, your calling(s), your destiny, and your responsibility.

As we allow our spiritual D.N.A. to identify us and as we allow ourselves to be blessed, we release blessings from our heart's thoughts, which gives permission to our environment to bless us.

The Lord loves us too much to answer some of our prayers.

If you are going to pray, speak the word or don't pray.

Often God tells us about the beginning and the end, but the middle we walk out by faith.

As a couple, you can be unequally yoked in more than spirituality… there is intellect, thirst for God, belief in the supernatural, gifts of the spirit, callings, grooming and financial goals. Also, there can be inequality in the way individuals view child rearing. Know before you go.

Dysfunction fights God.

Ministry has its own culture, as does the game of golf. Not everyone will take time to understand and embrace either, the game or the calling.

God's promises are, at times, inexplicable phenomena, as is God Almighty. Only to be understood by peering into the word of the Lord and gaining from His revelatory insight.

Jesus did not waste time. Everything He did had purpose and He looked for an intentional outcome.

Jesus didn't just look at people's actions. He looked at their heart. So, it does matter what's in the heart.

Jesus knew those who were around Him. Do you?

What society calls setbacks aren't meant to stop your progress. Just reroute. Find another way. There is one!

Setbacks can make you crave success much more. Don't allow disappointments to keep you in the background forever. Rise up. God has your back!

God's blessings are available to all, but the receiver (us) decides which blessings they will take. We can refuse or accept them.

Once we trust the Lord, we have to allow God to work and stand back and see HIS salvation.

Do not get angry with God about what has not manifested in your life. You were told to ask and it shall be given. Did you ask?

God loves us enough to let us go.

God can appear to be 'last minute' but He is strategic.

Can you see the answers to your prayers even when nothing appears to be happening? When someone tells us they are pregnant, we believe them without any visible evidence of it. You can use the same faith to believe.

Have you really forgiven those who have hurt, betrayed or lied to or on you? Here is a test. If that individual or group needed food or water, would you be able to assist them without any malice aforethought?

When the Lord says, "Love your enemies," HE means exactly what, HE says. Love them. It is that simple.

No matter what happens in the world. God is still God.

You were not an accident. You were a part of a divine design for success.

Helping is a good thing but we can help too much. When the receiving party does not have the opportunity to overcome challenges for her/himself, we are helping too much.

Helping too much can cause the receiving party to be resentful towards the one helping.

Why is it that some human beings cannot wait to get "grown" but once they been there a while they may not welcome birthdays anymore?

Why rules and requirements are okay when it comes to others, but when we are held to the same, we call them unfair or antiquated?

Why do we learn how to take care of ourselves when we become sick?

Why is it okay for the preacher to preach/talk about other people's sins/wrongdoing/infractions, but ours are off-limits?

Why do people run from God when things are good and run to God when things are not so good?

Why do we continue to return to a job we hate to work with coworkers who do not understand who we are to receive a paycheck that is not enough?

Why is it that we can see clearly, what another person should do, while we sit back analyzing our own mess without getting answers?

Chapter 2: Encouragement

David encouraged himself in the Lord. King David had returned from a battle, only to find that his wives were gone, taken by an enemy, along with some of his men's wives. He was distraught. He sought the Lord and the Lord answered him. He was told he'd recover all. Afterwards, David encouraged himself.

Outside encouragement is good and needed, but when we can gain the inner strength with which to encourage ourselves, that is good, also. Who other than God and you know you any better? So, go ahead use your faith in God to encourage yourself! Sing, pray and talk to yourself. It is all okay and good.

You are better than your past mistakes, good enough to be present today and great for a tremendous future destiny.

You were meant for success. Don't listen to anyone who tells you otherwise.

You have greatness connected to you. It is in your D.N.A.

Your ideas are worth your attention.

You deserve good things.

You are worthy of being treated well.

It is okay to smile. Smiles keep some wrinkles at bay.

It is okay to treat yourself well.

Take care of you!

You were born to accomplish great things.

You can remove bad influences from your life.

You can love others, while loving yourself.

It is okay to speak up for yourself.

Even when it seems as if the world is falling down around your feet, you can still rise up!

It is okay to have a dream.

You have the right to be great!

You have capabilities that you have not tapped into as of yet.

Be observant. Remove things that cause depression!

Trust that inner feeling!

Some ideas are worth keeping close to the vest!

Do not allow anyone to put you down. You can stand up for yourself with assertiveness.

One of your ideas can change the world.

One of your ideas can change your life!

Do not accept what you do not want.

You do not have to stop where your parents stopped!

You are important to God!

This world needs you.

Your dreams can come true! They can and they will.

Your loyalty to yourself will be tested. Prepare and pass!

Even if you have lost everything, you can start better.

It is okay to encourage yourself.

It is okay to accept yourself!

It is okay to like yourself!

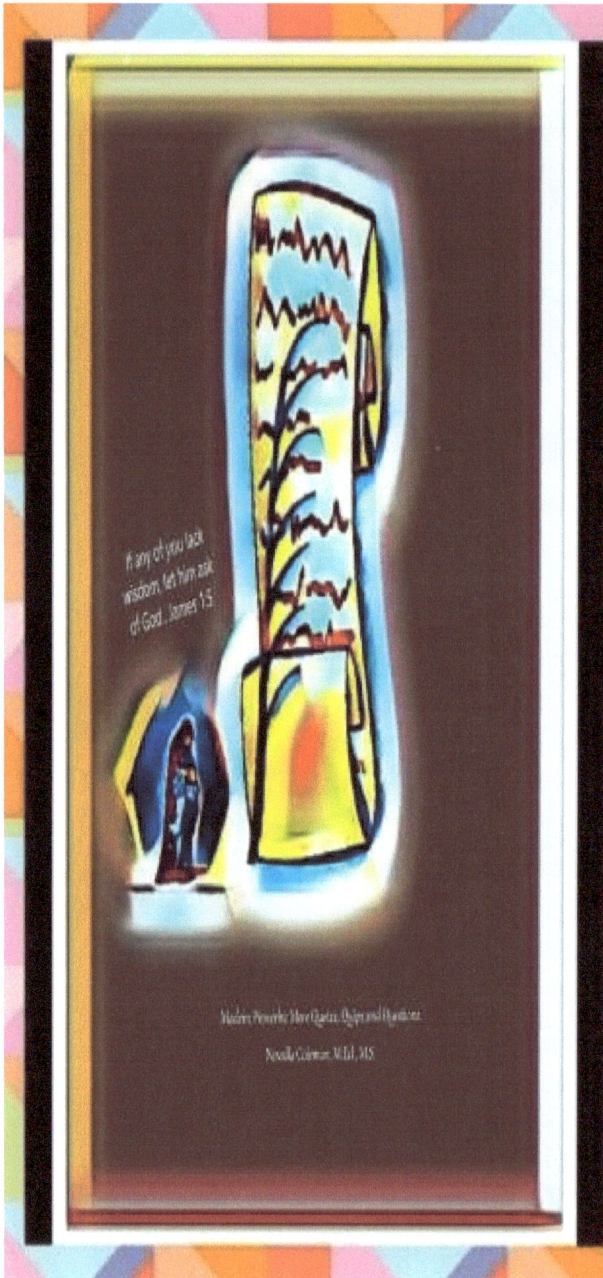

If any of you lack wisdom, let him ask of God...James 1:5.

Modern Proverbs: More Quotes, Quips and Questions

Novella Coleman, M.Ed., MS

"Ask" Wisdom

"Ask" Wisdom

Chapter 3: Ever Thought About This?

As a man thinketh, so is he

We possess a mind because we are to think. Therefore, it is okay to think. We have to think right thoughts, though. Our thoughts are important to our walk in Christ. What we think on and how we think determines what we do.

The scripture tells us this....Finally, brethren, whatsoever things are honest, whatsoever things are pure, whatsoever things are just, whatsoever things are lovely, whatsoever things are of good report; if there be any virtue, and if there be any praise, think on these things. Phil. 4:8. God made us and everything HE made is good.

Do not wait until you have noise to appreciate peace and serenity.

Refrain from the killer mentality and killer statements when others share their dreams with you.

There are many delivery systems in this world, but God delivers, too.

You do not have to give birth (physically) to be a mother

Take care of yourself. When you do not take care of yourself, you will not be able to take care of anyone else.

Not everyone is to remain in your life forever. Examine.

When a paper plate has been used for a meal, we usually do not go into the trash to retrieve it. This is a picture of some relationships. They were needed for a season and now, they are no longer good for anything except the trashcan. Let them go!

In most instances, individuals let us know who they are; we just choose to ignore who they are.

When you know you must move on, there are people who will have to be left behind as well.

We should focus more on attitude versus aptitude.

Do you break your promises and then wonder why no one keeps their word to you?

Can you trust yourself?

Do not allow people into your life who show you that they don't respect you. It is easier to keep them out versus eradicating them later.

Do not argue with others about what they believe. Only God and that person's own will can change what they believe. It is a waste of your most valuable time.

It is okay to be alone. It is temporary, if you want it to be.

There is always a way out, the bible declares it and it is so.

Just because it looks like there is, a brick wall in front of you doesn't mean there isn't a tunnel under it to the other side. Look for solutions.

One person or group creates recipes and someone else comes along and alters them to their own taste. It's the same with our circumstances. How can we overcome if we don't have something to overcome? We must alter the circumstances with our faith in God.

So teach us to number our days, that we may apply our hearts unto wisdom. Psalm 90:12 KJV

Then he said unto them, go your way, eat the fat, and drink the sweet, and send portions unto them for whom nothing is prepared for this day is holy unto our LORD: neither be ye Sorry, for the joy of the Lord is your strength. Nehemiah 8:10

Open your eyes. Awaken! Be who God called you to be.

Chapter 4: Ah Ha!

If any of you lack wisdom, let him ask of God, that giveth to all [men] liberally, and upbraideth not; and it shall be given him. James 1:5

See then that ye walk circumspectly, not as fools, but as wise. Ephesians 5:15-17

Ah Ha moments, as some call them, happen all around us. The challenge for some may be to remain awake enough to recognize the shift being made possible for the observant. May you remain conscious to what, when, who, how and why, when they show up in your atmospheric realm. You are possibilities here in human form. Take advantage, avail yourself to each one, as each ah ha is a teacher for the present and the future construction of your desired world.

When God allows us eye-opening revelations, we cannot be the same. We have been educated, truth revealed and so, we must use this new information to better our conditions and the condition of others.

In the Bible, we learned of blind Bartimeaus. Christ, our savior, healed him. Before Jesus healed him, he did not work, as he was blind. When our eyes become open, things change, the way we see things, literally and figuratively, changes. Ah-ha moments happen to us all of the time, but we choose to see or not see. Now for some quotes.

The attitude we adapt after, what seems to be a disappointment, reveals our true character.

The method with which we navigate disappointment shows whether we are truly strong.

Test before you invest.

Squatters are aggressors.

Ghetto is a state of mind not an address.

Some say money doesn't grow on trees; however, determining whether the fruit of a tree has monetary valuation is for the perspective eye of the beholder, as it were.

Fear is a rogue police officer, stopping those whom he should not.

Some so-called *loners* are those who have been betrayed and now, are afraid of companionship.

A person can be fired from anything, a marriage, a position, a friendship, a university.

When one becomes cognizant of one's desirability where it relates to receiving blessings, openness enters the heart and mind.

Men were designed to give; however, boys are selfish.

Some want your expertise without your experience or without experiencing you!

A scarred heart is a closed heart.

A scarred heart is a fragile heart.

What is valued is protected; it is neither lost nor misplaced, neither is it left unsupervised or with the unreliable.

Our strongest desires offer realized manifestations. The things we don't want leave our lives in time. This testifies to the strength of the human will and thoughts.

We cannot possess what we are not. Even if we appear to possess the thing or idea, we will lose possession, eventually.

Promotion can take place on many different planes.

Promotion begins in the mindset and consciousness reality.

Our promotion is, at times, a promotion up out of something. A new job, more responsibility in the present one or into a better position in life, a set-up.

In relationships, we cannot be one in our money, if we are not one in our honey…

To live you must put forth effort.

What you don't control will eventually control you.

Faith is a highway.

Organized chaos means things look out-of-place to others but the organizer can go right to the needed item.

It takes time to do excellence. It is not a microwave process.

You know you've made it when your *ex* comes to see your show. Alternatively, could it be that they want to stop supporting you? Therefore, they need to see how big you really are so the lawyer can stop the alimony checks because, clearly, you are self-sufficient.

Where there is lack of diversity there is increased susceptibility to illness: no diversity equals weakness.

Lack of diversity is insanity because it limits the exercise of a free exchange of ideas.

Don't get entangled in the monotony of everyday and stuck, while the long-term things slip through your fingers.

Now, some personal characteristics seem small and insignificant when love and desire fill the hearts and the minds of those involved. However, it is inevitable that those personal characteristics will come to the forefront as time progresses.

Sometimes, what we hold onto is only a hindrance.

Some people try to make a roadmap for your life and they don't know where *you're* headed.

Some people try to make a roadmap for your life and they don't know where *they're* headed.

When you become disconnected from the Source, you become static-filled, abnormal, disjointed, and distorted.

You cannot become what you are unable to envision for yourself. See bigger, brighter, better for yourself.

Those who seem to be with you today, but who are against you tomorrow, and against you the next day were not really with you at all. Don't get lulled into comfort and complacency. They might just be an enemy after all. Spies always try to infiltrate to learn the inside strategies so they can take the other side down.

People may only show their internal and intellectual possibilities when they're up against what appears to be impossibilities.

You are already what you can envision for your life, but it is in seed form. Allow it to grow.

If men ever had to experience 9 months of pregnancy and all of its glory, babies would be born instantaneously and pregnancy would come with a lot more perks.

If men had to have a cycle, the cycle would be no more. It would be eliminated.

If men had to have a mammogram, there would be a revolutionary method to assist medical practitioners in determining who is at risk.

Another observation, the people in the "hood" have been unemployed for years, haven't been able to take a trip, a real one, a vacation. They live and die within 2 square miles of their birthplace. And amazingly, they never think of jumping off a bridge, shooting themselves or doing suicide by car. So, they are jobless, behind on their bills or child support, have no health insurance and yet their clothes are always neatly pressed, hair in place, and such. Oh, and they smell good.

One who performs his or her duty is not owed any congratulatory remarks; however, ample appreciation is warranted.

Every day, you are a teacher in the life of someone else. Be sure the lessons are wholesome and worthwhile.

A beautiful dance can be performed as a solo but some dances require a skillful partner to bring out the hidden beauty. Be open to relationships.

A house may represent the occupants' salaries, while a home represents the occupants' tranquility and love for each other.

The person who is able to tell you the truth without regard to your feelings may be a true friend.

When you reach the top: don't forget what and who got you there.

Sometimes, the greatness of our strength is demonstrated in our gentleness.

Stop trying to be another person's perfect and be your own perfect!

Tears at funerals are for the living not the dead!

Funerals are for the living not for the departed. The living need the funeral to say good-bye because the departed are done here on the earth.

My attitude about money should not be…look at what I spent but look at what I've accomplished.

We water our plants more than we water ourselves.

If we treated our spouses the way most people treat their bosses, there would be no divorce.

The fearless person goes past the barricades, the barbed wire fence, the security gate, and all other seeming obstacles in life.

The graveyard has no mercy.

The graveyard has no comedy.

The graveyard has no future.

Some females thought they had a relationship but they had been violated!

When you have the cognitive mental playground of a wealthy individual, you will have the material, tangible playground of the wealthy…eventually.

I attract what is most prevalent within the inner recesses of my being and not what is resident in my outer package wrapping.

That which you want to eliminate from your future needs eradicated from your present.

When you wish betterment for a group or an individual and put the mental and physical energy into that endeavor, you will reap the rewards in the form of your personal betterment.

If you don't like your *outcome*, you need to alter the *income* of your thoughts and mind.

Don't attempt to change your friends and loved ones; change yourself and the caliber of your friends and your loved ones will automatically change.

Dream big! Need I say more?

I speak life into my words and words into my life.

I speak words into my life and life into that which I want to live on.

When a person cannot follow instructions, they will begin to lose everything… they've been given.

When someone doesn't consider you or your wants and desires, they are demonstrating their level of care for you.

Dysfunction can lead to an unavoidable death sentence.

Dysfunction is not pleasing to the senses.

Dysfunction is costly.

Dysfunction is an indication of dishonor.

Dysfunction is painful.

Dysfunction wastes time.

Dysfunction causes pain.

Life in some of its various forms: Alive and Healthy. Alive and unhealthy. Sickness and disease. Coma. Life support. Brain dead. Physical Death.

In a relationship, the parties are committed to one another; however, the eyes see other beautiful and/or handsome and admirable creations. These are unavoidable. It is the second, third and fourth look, and so on that can be troublesome. Reel it in.

A "thank you" is not enough for some, who have given so much of themselves in time, talent and tangibles. Try to blow their minds with your reciprocity.

Your actions can cause someone to like you. It is love that requires no action on the part of the receiver. Love is a gift you give away.

Are unemployment figures correct? If someone has been unemployed 10 years and there is no unemployment check, are they still counted? Probably not!

Submission to the Lord causes a continual maintenance of access, timely conclusions and a divine security system that provides 24/7 protection.

The one who feeds the nation my soon rule that same nation.

Always understand what another person's assistance will cost. There is always a cost.

Ever been in a relationship where one party is angry or *snaps* quite frequently? When asked about this, the other party says, "I am not angry!" Did you buy that? Anger in another person is very noticeable. It is an attitude, change in behavior, habits, friendships, and activities. Pay attention. Anger is a sign!

Have you ever heard someone who has what they call *bad luck*, it seems to happen, continually? Listen to them; they are calling bad luck, bad breaks, and such into their world. They keep saying they have it and it keeps coming to answer their call. Watch them and observe carefully, what they call will manifest for them. It is a law!

Be yourself. There is no one…absolutely…just like you. Even twins have differences, although, they are ever so slight. God created you as an individual. So be one!

Admiration is not bad. Don't get obsessed with stars and celebrities; they are human beings with a pulse and a home address. Don't worship them. They are not immortals!

Don't be surprised when aunts, cousins, and uncles shun you. This can be a sign of greatness.

You cannot be a negative person inside and have positive results on the outside.

Don't be afraid to discipline your children, but do it while they are in the kneecap crowd. Bigger children; bigger challenges.

No one gets away with anything. The all-powerful, almighty Creator takes account of everything done here by humans. Don't be fooled. You will reap your actions, so be loving and kind and do unto everyone, as you would have them do unto you.

Value creativity.

Value courage.

Value honesty.

Value good health.

Let the intent in your eyes be guided by the Lord. This way, you can see right.

It's okay to declare what you want. No one can give you an, "I don't know."

In life, there are many choices to make and only you can make them!

Don't get upset about how beautiful someone else is, how successful they are, or even who they have as a mate, because you have no idea of what they've had to go through, what they are experiencing now, and what they may have to encounter. So, be thankful for your stuff, how you look, and whom you were privileged to marry. If you knew what the other person's life and experiences were, you might want to keep your own life and the relationships you have.

Ladies, sisters and friends character is not built with bricks and mortar; it is built with overcoming difficulties, saying no to things you would normally say yes to, holding your peace when you want to curse someone and tell them, just a little bit, about themselves, and refraining from slapping the mess out of a co-worker, for instance.

In life, you get what you anticipate and focus upon.

How many of you are a part of a couple, you have a significant other, or such? Couples who are in-sync with one another are like a classical symphonic musical rendition; there is not one *off* beat in the entire piece.

If the other person in the relationship is not important; soon, there will be no relationship.

A relationship will be lost when one person is not valued.

When you continuously avoid and/or delay going home, you need to find out what you are afraid of or what you don't want to deal with and why you avoid making the trip.

What is free to you may cost me everything.

When I take responsibility for my part in past failure, I can take my power back and begin to move forward with newness of revelation.

Allowing others to make decisions for you is for those who are void of ambition.

Allow others to speak as much as is possible because people always tell us who they are if we would only listen and take heed.

Only what you are at the core of your being will come to fruition in your life. Are you life or death, hate or love, free or shackled?

Length of speech doesn't necessarily translate into quality of speech.

Don't discount a blind man; he may have more sight then most…like insight and foresight.

Those who dance with the Lord....always have a faithful partner.

Those who run with God never lose the race.

Dreams are the fuel for life.

Although happiness is a wonderful state of being, it is a temporary state of being.

Love is an action word.

God is the ultimate coach...listen to his words. You will know the next move.

Prophecy is the intimacy of whispers from the lips of God.

Deal with any challenge by following the passion of Christ....See the goal and finish it. You will rise again!

Remember to use your TAGS...Talents, Abilities, Gifts!

Some relationships are like upside down real estate, there is more invested in them then they are worth.

Resurrection brings assurance.

Lifers have abandoned all other options.

Some actions cannot be done simultaneously with equal precision.

God is the master recycler. He takes our junk and makes it into beauty.

If all things work together for good, why do we want to pick and choose what event we'll welcome and the ones we'll refuse and return to sender?

Once you have raised your children, you'll have to trust the God in them to do what is right.

The assignment may be big, but you have a God who has no limits. So, go on and do big things with God leading the way!

Never think anything good or evil is left unnoticed. God sees it all. Each will receive what is due.

Even when it looks like everything is falling apart, don't give up.

Try one more time; this time it may work. Do it another way, maybe your idea needs new life.

Those people and things that we do not appreciate will depreciate out of our lives.

Still talking about it? Don't be fooled. It is still relevant to them and they are not over it!

What you allow..allows more of the same. Stop it while it's a pebble before it becomes a boulder.

Chapter 5: Joy. Laughter. Happiness

What can I say here? We can laugh, be happy and have joy, if we so choose. It is up to us. When God tells us, "According to your faith, be it done unto you." He means just that. If we don't have certain things, it's not God, it's us.

Real joy comes from the inward sanctum of a life that is balanced with the Divine.

Joy delights.

Joy frees.

Joy reveals.

Joy creates.

Joy grows.

Joy pleases.

Joy invites.

Joy intoxicates.

Joy renews.

Joy fertilizes.

Laughter cleanses.

Laughter liberates.

Laughter gathers.

Laughter reveals.

Laughter overcomes.

Laughter creates.

Laughter shares.

Laughter rewards.

Laughter rejuvenates.

Laughter heals.

Laughter connects.

Happiness can be concealed; unhappiness cannot.

Happiness begets happiness.

Happiness creates its own level.

It is not good enough to just dream.

Inflexibility is the main ingredient in broken relationships including divorce.

Attempting to assassinate those called by God, through verbal or physical means, leads to spiritual incarceration in the areas of finance, success, freedom and happiness.

Creativity unused is like a lover who never expresses their true feelings; it brings frustration, unhappiness and loss.

Staying with someone out of habit is a life of drudgery and misery for both parties; only true love can bring joy and happiness.

Un-forgiveness is like an unpaid debt.

Un-forgiveness keeps you bound in the past.

Since the root system of some trees are as wide in circumference as the widest part of the length of the branches at the top. Watch the outside or actions you will get a glimpse at the roots inside of another person.

Tattoos can be the hieroglyphics for those who feel unvoiced.

A nation that doesn't value education will soon lose its financial wealth.

You have to be a husband before you are one!

Don't marry a man who is old enough to be your father unless you are prepared to have one.

A male who wants his wife or significant other to take financial pressure off him is not ready to be a man.

One who makes God a priority will make you a priority.

Silence speaks to us…if we are willing to listen.

We can educate the world…one student at time.

Successful students are a planned phenomenon.

We share our life with others….in death we are alone.

In life, we have to share; in death, it is okay to be selfish.

Even those who are unable to speak need to hear how much we love them.

Just because you only know her, as your mother doesn't mean she is not complex and multi-faceted.

When you deny the Great Destiny that has been ordained for you by God, you deny God who is the mastermind.

In life, there is not a *true* middle ground called compromise: there is black and white, yes or no, in or out.

For the successful, there is no middle ground; there is decision.

Picking a fight with a giant guarantees notoriety, the audience of those in authority and new and influential relationships.

God doesn't require an intermediary to get a message to one who is attuned to his voice.

When you swim with the fishes, you cannot soar with the eagles.

One who is unable or unwilling to value customers has no business being in business and will soon be out of business because they do not see customers as an integral part of their business and the reason they are in business in the first place.

The stingy will always be in poverty in some area of their life.

There is a cost to education; it is priceless.

You cannot be king of the Castle when you don't own a home of your own.

Make room for increase

We should be like God, in that, he always prepares for the next thing. He is prepared.

One who is able to share is not a prisoner of that which he shares. He is free and not owned by anyone or anything he possesses.

You are not your looks.

And the *eyes* have it, remember to look into other people's eyes they are a display cabinet for the soul.

God's system never has a "crash."

God's system never gets a "virus."

God's system never requires a virus scan.

God's system never requires an upgrade or a reboot.

Even if I decide to do nothing, I have still made a decision.

I can set the tone of my day.

Even the botanical world demonstrates the beauty and necessity for diversity. A lesson can be learned from a bouquet of flowers.

That which is stagnate breeds takers, scavengers and uncleanness.

Stagnation has no beauty.

Stagnation creates illness and death.

Stagnation has a distinguishable smell.

That which is stagnate is not fit for enjoyment.

Stagnation has a purpose.

Stagnation creates isolation.

That which is stagnant is unsightly.

Low self-esteem is ungodly.

Low self-esteem is a personal abuse of self.

Low self-esteem draws abusers to your life.

Low self-esteem stunts personal growth.

Low self-esteem is rooted in lies.

Low self-esteem creates self-denial.

Low self-esteem brings dreams to a halt.

Low self-esteem encapsulates creativity.

Low self-esteem kills.

Low self-esteem chars the consciousness.

Hatred blinds.

Hatred kills.

Hatred lies.

Hatred binds.

Hatred detours.

Hatred curses.

Hatred is bitter.

Hatred is painful.

Hatred pollutes.

Hatred depresses.

Hatred repels.

Even stagnation creates…it creates a state of sickness (illness, crippling) and death.

God has a 24/7 help desk.

Death creates….it creates a vacuum, sadness, joy, tears, stench, actions, and reactions.

It is expensive to attempt to be someone you're not; you sell yourself short, lose your identity, devalue what your creator did, and cheat the world out of the wonders of YOU!

When the people who are closest to you are no longer pleasing to you, take an introspective look at yourself because the outward life of an individual begins with the inside.

Commitment equals character.

Men need to be needed.

The patient ones have real strength.

A man who begins to feel inferior to the primary female in his life will soon look for a female to whom he feels superior or at least equal.

Men who feel emasculated will seek out females who make them feel like men. She builds him up.

Men who do not want a physical relationship with their wives are either not attracted to her any longer, not attracted to females, battling an illness or dysfunction, or are deriving pleasure elsewhere.

Relationship and selfishness should not be in the same sentence.

Tears flush.

Tears cloud.

Tears close.

Tears heal.

Tears divide.

Tears identify.

Tears cover.

Tears drown.

Tears sell.

Tears clear.

Those who don't maintain the home may not see themselves as long-term tenants or owners thereof.

Life is a multiple-choice situation: after choices are made, life is like a maze. Once inside the maze: life becomes a multiple-choice situation, again.

Enemies appear before promotion.

Creativity brings victory.

In a marital relationship with God, God is never the estranged person, in that, God changes not. Thus, he could never be the estranged party. Check your own status.

Those who are in a state of unrestraint in expressing their unsolicited opinions may be selfish and prideful.

Those who are unable to be themselves are consistently cheating themselves and society.

If you have to hold back from the one you profess to love; examine yourself, your love may not be real or you may not love them.

When you consistently give, you consistently receive.

Those who continuously take will continuously lose.

When you can control the tone and course of your words, you can control the tone and course of your life's path.

Inattention to ideas stops the flow of ideas from coming through like a dam is to water flow.

Creativity causes prosperity.

As human beings, we cannot stop time but we can redeem time by yielding to the *One* who has time in His hands.

You have guaranteed growth when you take the posture of a student.

A student is one who has respect for all who are teachers; who they see in everyone they meet.

There is never competition when you are loved.

The genius of creativity is uncontainable. It will seep out somehow.

Money can buy many things, but it cannot buy peace of mind.

Creativity bridled is an enslaved prisoner; it will seek freedom at any cost even its own demise.

Creativity untapped is like an unclaimed inheritance; it becomes useless to one who really owns it.

Creativity is a blank check backed by a multi-billionaire.

Creativity brings clarity.

Creativity is profitable.

Creativity brings balance.

Creativity is a gift from God.

Creativity is power to change.

Betrayal leads to financial ruin.

Betrayal leads to emotional bankruptcy.

Betrayal leads to self-destruction.

Betrayal leads to severed relationships.

Betrayal leads to infamy.

Betrayal reveals its gateway and entry point.

Creativity brings favor.

No matter how difficult, God can deliver.

Remember Black Slaves, the Children of Israel and the Berlin Wall. Things can change.

Creativity reveals your enemies.

Reassess your relationships.

Don't tell someone you care about them and leave the *care-evidence* out of the equation.

One's caring cannot be hidden and it cannot be a drone. Caring is always demonstrable.

Boys become flustered at what men find fascinating.

Don't try to save the drowning world at large, while your loved ones are awaiting the flood at home.

Some believe that the mind (thinking) and body (physical) are separate....but where the mind or thinking venture; the body will, eventually, experience the adventure.

You cannot reason with a demoniac.

You cannot reason with a drunken man.

A vacation is not always a place but it can be a feeling, too. Human beings spend money, time, and lots of energy for a feeling!

When a man is in perpetual youth, he is neither child nor man.

Some individuals can be a drain on your life like a cell phone searching for a signal. You can only change locations to be connected to a strong signal. Allow the thing to die (draining relationship) or somehow plug into a source (non-draining, encouragement) that will keep the battery consistently charged.

Some will not reach their full potential until we let go of them!

Be cautious about counting folks out. God may be using the new math and your calculations may be all wrong!

Never believe that you, alone, are the reason for someone else's success, remember, God is the almighty one.

People show us how they really feel about us; we just fail to recognize the signs or we don't want to recognize them because there are always signs.

Love is like an obstacle course; the one who persists wins the "love" prize.

Love is a cool breeze on a hot day.

Faith has perfect timing.

Faith has no panic within.

Faith is not afraid of the word…no.

Faith doesn't fear death.

Love lasts forever.

Love makes one feel safe and gives one the ability to be transparent.

You cannot kill love

Love never turns into hate but hate can turn into love.

Having more space doesn't mean you have more room, if limitations still exist in the psyche.

God is a God of peace and prosperity even when your life appears to indicate the opposite.

You cannot change a liar from the outside.

Teaching someone how to care is like teaching someone to breathe; by the time, they're ready to be taught, they should have already learned.

Fighting the process is like boxing the air; you are fighting in vain and swinging on the invisible.

A female without a visible soft side is a well and a wall of pain.

When you hold onto things, you may become like a trash can, which holds on to all of the trash (negative words, titles and judgment) that others dish out or throw in.

Some people are afraid to follow the bible, but they will follow a recipe to the letter.

When I pondered the lives of the rich, I understood how one becomes the "I am" of a thing. The rich believe they belong already. They feel deserving of the thing, they are there and that's a given. It is only a matter of time.

Good leaders are those who can tell you "no" and make you believe it was your idea!

Leaders are not always born. The heat of life's tests, melt them into shape and press them out by the "iron" of adversity.

Good leaders listen.

Leaders know how to give orders without yelling, belittling or intentionally hurting their team or team members.

Good leaders are great communicators.

Strong leaders can fire someone in a heartbeat, size someone up in a blink, make a deal with a handshake, and walk away from a mistake and start again just like it never happened.

Leaders constantly prepare for the future.

Good leaders know their weaknesses.

Good leaders know their strengths.

Good leaders do not run from challenges.

Good leaders are creative problem solvers.

When we see others correctly, they are not known by their race. They are known by their character.

Rewards don't follow thoughts. Rewards follow actions.

Future life is designed from past and present thoughts.

You may not be the fastest, the prettiest, the strongest, the most influential but you can be the best *you* and greatest human being who ever lived.

If others propose imperfection as a resolution to your needs, their feelings for you also, may be imperfect.

When you love someone everything they do is good, cute, funny, precious, eccentric, beautiful, and *outside the box,* while when you do not love someone everything they do is bad, odd, ugly, distasteful, weird, and simply crazy.

God is our *Source.* Other human beings are only a resource.

Immature males do not mind being dependent and are content, while mature men, on the other hand want to be and are content with, and seek out situations and relationships where they can be the one who is depended upon.

Garbage cans bring the garbage man. Don't be a garbage can.

A selfish and cheap male is not husband material.

Humans tend to stay young who stay around the young.

Why do you want God to keep the thing going and finish it, when HE did not ordain the thing in the first place?

Plan for tomorrow, but live in today.

When God tells us to move on, we may be misunderstood, but the blessing is in the doing!

If you love your neighbor but hate your children, examine your love for yourself. Your children are like looking at a reflection of yourself.

Trusting God is like a recipe for success.

Trusting God is like riding on a train as it goes through twists, turns, changes tracks, goes through dark tunnels, and under bridges. The conductor sees everything before you do. They know which turns to make and which track is best to get everyone to their desired destination. And when it's dark, they already know the outcome for you. You have to stay aboard and **finish** the ride.

Sometimes, you cannot explain the will of God. You just know it to be true!

When you feel you don't belong in something, you cannot have real peace.

When you feel like you belong, you act like it!

Possession of many books does not make one a scholar.

Thinking about accomplishment and performance of that accomplishment are related but are not one and the same.

Just because it is in the garbage doesn't make it trash.

You cannot have real change if you have an invisible mask or costume on your person. First, the mask or costume must be removed and then, the change is revealed.

Sometimes, a marriage is like a coffin. Someone got inside and died.

We are always *somebody* to God, but until we pursue our God-given destiny, we are *a nobody* to society. Pursuit of destiny=we become somebody to the world.

We are always important to God, even when we seem to slip into obscurity amongst everyone else.

When we do not do what we can; eventually, we cannot do what we want.

Making someone else pay for the hurts of our past is like a police person ticketing the person who obeyed the law, while the speeder gets away clean

If the earth is 2/3 water, is there water in the Mojave and the Sahara?

Being too comfortable can be dangerous.

Each day is a seed and a harvest.

Everyone is a seed and harvest, a seed to one person is a harvest to another.

All lawful pleasures are to be enjoyed in moderation, so as not to produce addiction.

Maybe the reason a person can't sleep well at night is that they did not do what was right in the daylight!

Is it true that all alcoholics have unresolved anger inside?

Why do people kill themselves with substances?

Why do some groups call themselves Anonymous when everyone knows why everyone and anyone is there?

Don't listen to people when they tell you they can deal with anything. Watch their actions. Tell them "no" or "I cannot do that for you" and see where they go with that!

If you are a teacher…then teach. Don't make would be students pay with belittling comments, bullying episodes, your tirades, and your ineffectiveness. Step aside and let the real teachers enter the classroom.

Learn everything you can from your experiences. You will need the information later. God always prepares you for the next event. Don't let anything go to waste!

Marriage is not about what you get, it is about what you give.

If you take care of others better than you do your own family, you are foolish because you can't go HOME to the other people in your life.

When you treat your wife or husband as an insignificant party, she/he will become an insignificant party in your life by exiting.

When you cherish others, they feel it and they will seek you out even if it costs them everything.

Where you spend your time and money tells others what and whom you love.

You can always be a better you than anyone else.

When considering a goal, focus on the benefits not the barriers.

It is important to have loyalty in relationships. One person who is with you is better than thousands who are just hanging around you.

Friendship is proven in the time of need.

Don't tell me what you believe, demonstrate.

What you hear you will eventually say.

Adversity is like a juice extractor, it will squeeze the true intentions out.

Putting yourself down is like pouring last week's garbage on all over yourself.

Putting one's self down is a form of hiding.

Putting yourself down is like stabbing yourself in the back.

Putting yourself down is self-sabotage.

Good communication skills are imperative. My right is your left. My here may be your there. So, make sure the other person understands what you are trying to say.

Some despise what you love and some love what you despise. Embrace it and let it be.

Alone and lonely are not one and the same. Alone is a physical state, while lonely is a mental state. Choose wisely.

The people who do not value you do not belong in your life.

People say, "Don't forget where you came from," but I say, "Don't forget where you are going, either." Focus, Focus, Focus.

When you *make it* don't forget about God!

When a relationship loses its usefulness, discard it.

People know when you genuinely care about them.

When it seems like you have nothing, you have the most because that's when your real wealth, your creativity, comes alive.

There is never a shortage. It only looks like it and that is an illusion. Just keep looking and don't give in to negativity.

Assuming can put one's life in danger.

Solutions can be simple and right in front of us. The search, research and development is daunting.

Your children mirror you in some way.

Try to love people for who they are on the inside and not the outside. The inside is who they are, their outside changes and can be altered by surgery and injections.

Children are not born with a belief that they are ugly. It takes another human being to do that work.

It takes God to create human beings but it takes human beings to turn them into animals.

Don't judge your life by the adversities you've experienced but by what you have overcome.

It is a mystery how human beings can kill another human being just because they have the power to do so.

Some people believe they can't do something because they have not put forth the effort to do whatever that something is.

When human beings are forced to act, they discover inner strength and hidden gifts

Don't determine your wealth consciousness by the negative balance in your bank account.

Larvae may look grotesque right now but wait until it is a butterfly before you judge.

Don't let the process scare you away. Usually beautiful cakes start out as batter and have to be mixed, stirred and guided into the right situation (a pan or mold) by a master (baker) before beauty (finished product) arrives.

Because your destiny is great, some people will exit your life. Let it happen. They were never meant to stay. They shall be replaced. Let them release the space. Focus on the positive things in your life. If you remember they don't belong to you and they don't belong with you, you will be able to see those that do belong to you and with you.

No one is irreplaceable but they may be a little different. Accept.

When you focus on solutions, the problem will not overwhelm you.

When one season ends, you have to shift or you will be out-of-sync with what's next and out-of-season.

Be thankful.

Smell the flowers. Observe the trees. Listen to the music. Hear the children laugh. Enjoy.

Remain engaged and attentive in your own life.

Watch for signs of changing seasons. Signs always exist.

Do you know when someone is letting go?

Are you aware of yourself?

Do you consider your words before you release them into the atmosphere?

Pay attention to the uttered words of others. We cannot say what we have not thought upon in mind.

Shield your mind. Your mouth will tell the world where you have been in thought.

There may be times when it is better to have few words of meaning than to spew empty, poison and word lashes with the tongue. Only to regret most of them later.

When someone asks you to have a few words, have a few.

When your dream life manifests, you'll need gas for the car, and a way to upkeep the house.

Pride is funny. It'll have you blind until it's too late. Stop and reflect. Ask yourself, why am I doing this and for whom?

It costs nothing to enjoy God's creation. Stop and smell the flowers and watch the bumblebee.

If the teacher is a bully, how can the children learn?

It costs to care but the rewards are exponential.

Would you still do it if just one person's life changed?

Don't ask God how He will answer your prayer(s). Just know as you prayed according to God's will, your prayer will be answer in divine time. You can ask God to help you to understand something and He, as our SOURCE, will guide you to the resources required to understand and overcome. So, continue to trust HIM. *N.C*

Chapter 6: Why?

I am one who will ask God why. Some say, I am wrong for asking. I say, "Why can't I ask the ONE, who has all of the answers?" It makes no sense to me to ask someone else when I can go directly to the ONE, who knows. Anyway, I, like many others, have been told to pray but don't ask God why but I am walking this walk. So, I will continue to question. Don't get me wrong, there is no disrespect meant. God knows me. I just need to know and understand as much as He allows and I will ask. He designed me with an inquisitive mind and I will not change unless God requires it of me and without further ado, here are some whys.

Why do we worry? Worry never changes the situation. It never has and it never will.

Why do people travel far and near to get what they have in front of them. Assess. Assess. Assess.

Why do parents curse their own children? Don't they know that these miniatures are part of themselves? Hmmmm.

Why do we criticize our employer and continue to enter into their office or into their plant?

Why do we hate other races? Take a D.N.A. test, you may find that you hate yourself.

Why do we buy beautiful homes only to leave them for 10-12 hours a day?

Why do we come to God when we are about to expire?

Why do we act friendly towards people who we tear to shreds when they leave the room?

Why do we have imagination and faith for someone else's dream and our dream lies dormant within?

Why do we push away the ones who we claim to love?

Why be a fake? You cannot fake caring. Either you care or you don't.

Why do we pull out all stops when our loved one threatens to exit and yet when they were available we counted them as unworthy of our time and attention?

Why do we fight to get what we say we want and then let go when things get tough?

Why do we complain about our relationships and continue in them?

Why are we tough on crime when someone else is in trouble?

Why do we use encryption when we make online purchases? Only to turn around and tell anyone who will listen or read....we are out-of-town or out of the country including house numbers, hotel locations, and other details?

Why do we spend 40 hours at a job we hate?

Why do we cover for our child and make everyone else's child out to be a bad guy for the same or like infractions?

Why do we mistreat the poor?

Why do we take advantage of the disabled?

Why do we belittle other races unless we need them for something?

Why do we send our children to school and refuse to help them with their learning?

Why do we neglect our girls and celebrate our sons?

Why do we marry for convenience and divorce due to inconvenience?

Why do we take vacations to other cities and stay in and around the hotel?

Why do we buy bikes but never ride them?

Why do we pay for memberships and never use them?

Why do we order salads and drown them in dressing?

What is the point of having nice things and leaving them in the closet with the tags still on?

Why do we pay hundreds or thousands to a counselor or psychiatrist and ignore their advice?

Why do we buy a flat screen T.V. and put on 3-D glasses?

Why is it that the folks in the "hood" are so resilient? We hear of those in media who get embroiled in scandal, shoot themselves, jump off bridges, and do the suicide thing by exhaust fumes. On the other hand, the folks in the "hood" seem to live and live and die of ordinary heart disease.

Why do companies advertise free this and free that? As soon as contact is made, money is requested or a card number.

Why do we leave our childlike faith? It is that childlike faith, which informed us that there were no limits. It takes adults with their reason and logic to eradicate childlike faith. For it is the tainted in faith and adults who live INSIDE life's limits.

Why do we give up at the wrong time? If you've been waiting for something, keep watching and waiting. Don't throw in the towel. Don't give up!

Why do we lie to ourselves…about ourselves…within ourselves?

Why do we speak defeat and expect victory?

Why do we abuse the body and look for physical health?

Why do we mistreat children and then, require them to treat others right?

Why do we go easy on our children and expect them to deal with the hard things in life?

Why do we crucify others when they error and excuse our children and the people we know when they do the same things?

Why do we work to change our laws when they affect our families and us but leave unfairness on the books for the rest of the world?

Why do we say we judge by the content of character when we judge by everything else? Financial status, education, skin tone, address, hair, height and weight.

Why do we wait until we have a terminal diagnosis to forgive and let go?

Why do we bury the dead but keep dead situations around us indefinitely?

Why do we do what we wish but tell others to obey the rules?

Why do we ask for respect from others when we do not respect ourselves?

Why do we love strangers and hate our own family members?

Why do we talk behind people's back, when we could help them by telling them what we say about them? On the other hand, are we being mean and there is no usefulness in our talk?

Why do try to kill what we don't understand?

Why do we lie in every area of our lives but swear on the bible when we go to court?

Why do we mistreat our own flesh and blood? Could it be that we hate ourselves?

Why do we buy off the rack and get upset 'cause everyone else did too?

Why do we trust the accountant and distrust the preacher?

Why do we marry our enemy and divorce our friend?

Why do we stay at luxury hotels and spend every other day in shambled housing?

Why do we seek God in crisis and run from Him when we are blessed?

Why do we belittle our work boss and praise the crime boss?

Why do swim in an ocean but drown in debt?

Why do we lie to people we should be truthful with and tell the truth to those who deserve lies?

Why do we protect our reputations and destroy our forests?

Why do we whiten our teeth and darken our skin?

Why do we fold into our batter and unfold events?

Why do we treat our lawns and mistreat our elders?

Why do we exercise our faith but become a couch potato?

Why do we walk on eggshells and run errands?

Why do we walk a tight rope and skip classes?

Why do we ride a lazy river but catch waves?

Why do we hold onto the old and reject the new?

Conclusion

At the end of it all, we must think. Our thoughts are powerful as well as the words we release into the atmosphere. We are responsible for the life we have.

Our faith must temper what we think and what we verbalize. We can have what we say and what we think will project onto the screen of our lives.

At this point, what can I say? I am done, for now. May God grant you wisdom. And whatever you do, please teach the children. Peace and blessings.

About the Author

Meet author, Novalla Coleman, who is also a poet, an aspiring songwriter, and a motivational speaker. She feels called by God to write, to encourage and to serve as a motivating voice in the world. Ms. Coleman would like to inspire others to pursue their God-given gifts, talents, and abilities.

Novalla Coleman was born to Oscar (William) and Betty Mae Wright in Brooke, IN. She grew up in a rural area called Pembroke, now known as Pembroke Township. This town is also known as Hopkins Park but locals and those who have resided there or have family there call her Hopkins, the 'Hoppity', and the country. Pembroke is approximately 60 miles southeast of Chicago and very near the Illinois/Indiana Stateline. Ms. Coleman resides in Illinois with her family.

Novalla Coleman credits God with her writing abilities and with making her books possible because *"with God all things are possible." Matt. 19:26.*

www.novallacoleman.com

Other Books by Novalla Coleman

Mosaic Reflections: In Poetic Context, a poetry compilation filled with original inspirational poems and reflections on life by Novalla Coleman. https://amzn.to/2s4Z55l

Mosaic Reflections: Just Me & Poetry, a second poetry compilation by author, poet, Novalla Coleman, begins with poetic meditations and conversations with God in chapter 1. In subsequent chapters, the poet continues to create paintings/pictures as a skilled artisan on a blank canvas (her book) with the art of words as colorful mediums. Her brush stokes (words) are thought-provoking poems meant for spiritual reflection, dialogue, mental reorganization, and inner healing. Ms. Coleman paints poetic word art into aesthetic expressions, portraits, abstracts, caricatures and narratives. https://amzn.to/2s2CmaZ

Modern Proverbs: Quotes, Quips, and Questions is Ms. Coleman's first book in the quotes and wisdom genre but not her last as she shares "downloads" from God. https://amzn.to/2x3ICUT

www.ingramcontent.com/pod-product-compliance
Lightning Source LLC
Chambersburg PA
CBHW041219270326
41931CB00005B/115